Preschool Skills

My Neighborhood

This book provides fun practice in readiness skills for early learners. An appealing theme engages the attention of children as they complete the carefully chosen activities. The activities, which have been designed to prepare children for school, provide practice in beginning math, visual skills, fine-motor skills, language, thinking skills, and more! Children will enjoy exploring concepts related to *My Neighborhood* through a variety of fun activities!

Skills in this book include:
Numbers • Shapes • Sizes • Visual perception
Thinking skills • Language • Classification
And more!

Written by **Kaori Crutcher** and **Vicky Shiotsu**

Cover illustration by **Georgene Griffin**

Illustrated by **Georgene Griffin, Joyce John, Patty McCloskey,** and **Gerry Oliveira**

FS132903 My Neighborhood
All rights reserved—Printed in the U.S.A.
Copyright © 2000 Frank Schaffer Publications, Inc.
23740 Hawthorne Blvd.
Torrance, CA 90505

ISBN 0-7682-0381-3

Table of Contents
Skills & Concepts

At the Toy Store

Count. Draw a line to the number.

3

1

2

5

4

Name _____

Deliver the Mail

Cut out, match, and paste.

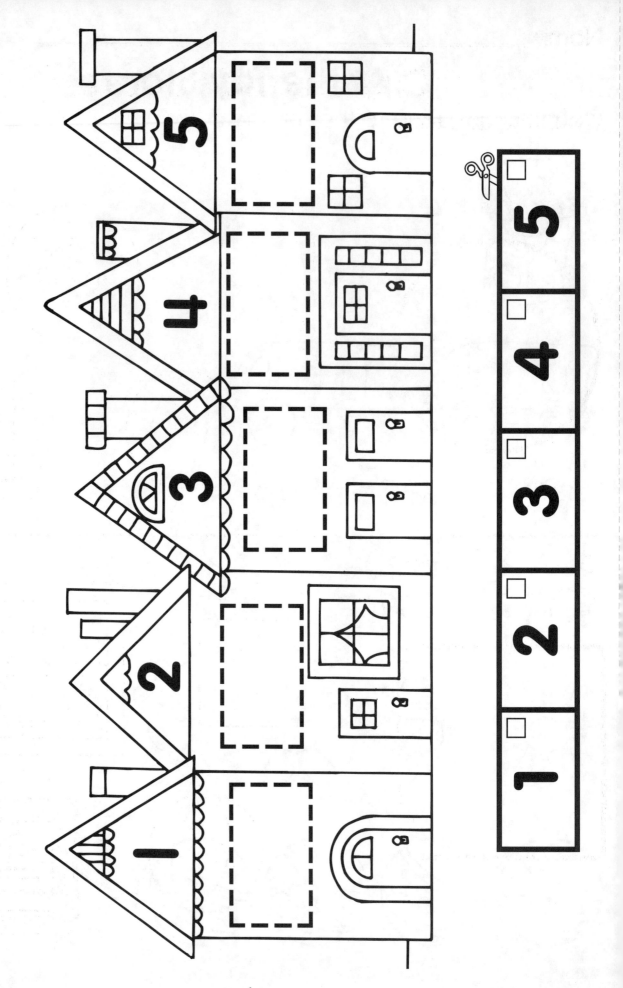

FS132903 My Neighborhood

Name _____

Circles and Squares

Color the circles.

Color the squares.

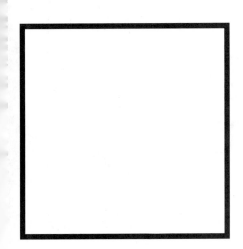
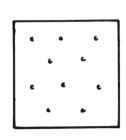

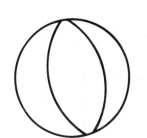

Triangles and Rectangles

Color the triangles.

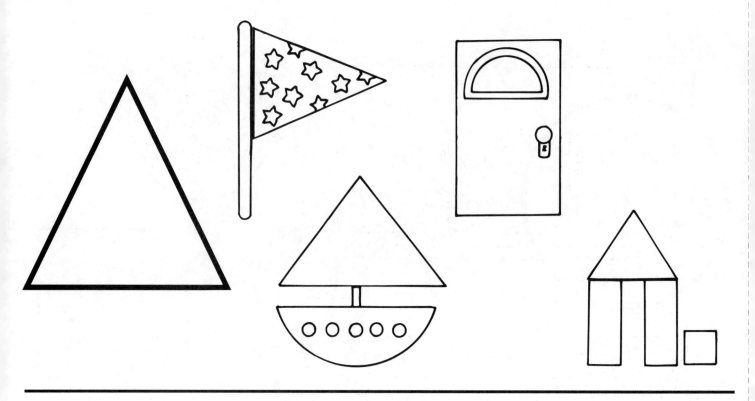

Color the rectangles.

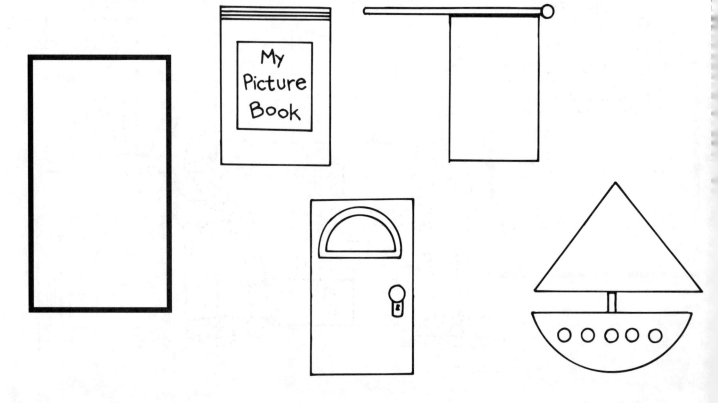

FS132903 My Neighborhood

Shapes at School

Color the circles, squares, triangles, and rectangles.

FS132903 My Neighborhood

Name _____

Visiting the Library

Help the child find the way to the library.

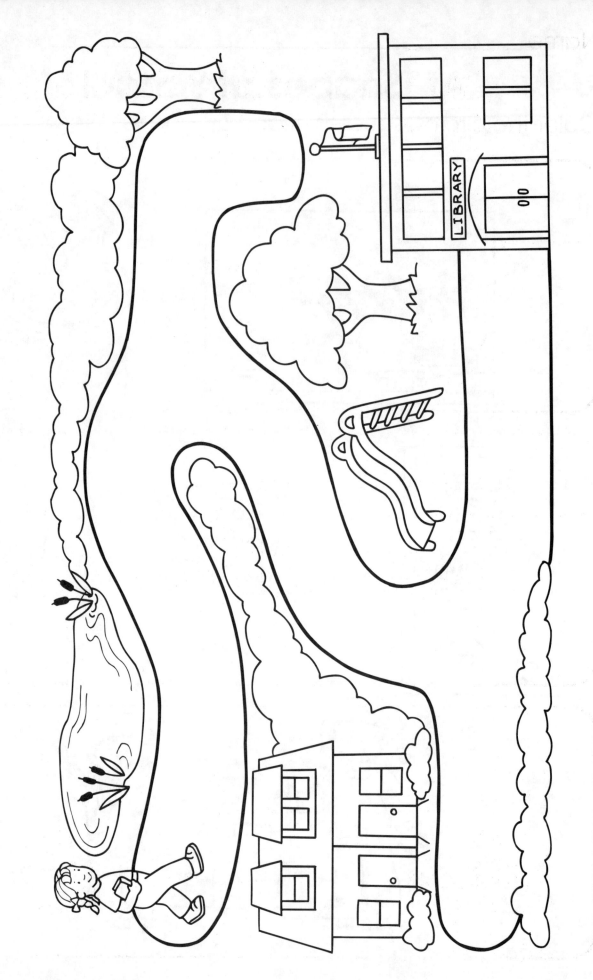

FS132903 My Neighborhood

At the Department Store

Color the smallest in each box.

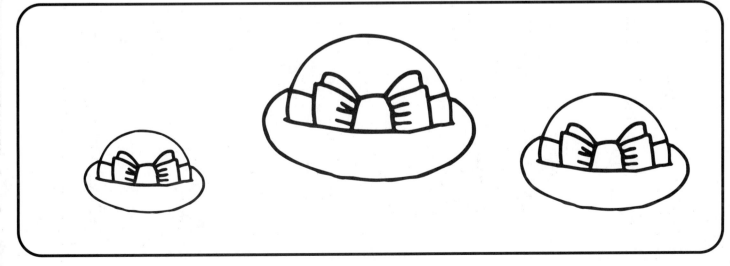

Same and Different

In each box, color the objects that are the same.

Shopping Time

Draw a line from each object to the matching store.

Name _____

My Neighborhood

Color and cut out.
Staple with page 13 to make a book.

My Book About My Neighborhood

I live in a neighborhood.

1

I play with my friends in a neighborhood.

2

FS132903 My Neighborhood

My Neighborhood

Color and cut out.
Staple with page 12 to make a book.

3

Mommy and I shop in our neighborhood.

4

Many people work in my neighborhood.

5

I can help keep our neighborhood clean.

FS132903 My Neighborhood

Name _____

Stop and Look

Find the (STOP) signs.
Color them red.

14

Skill: Classification

In the Neighborhood

Cut out the pictures and put them into three groups.
The groups are **Things That Go**, **Workers**, and **Places**.
Paste the groups to another sheet of paper.

Name _____

Police Officers Help Us

Help the police officer take the lost child home.

16

Name_____

Dress-Up Day

Cut out, match, and paste.

MAIL

17

Tool Time

rom each worker to the tool he or she needs.

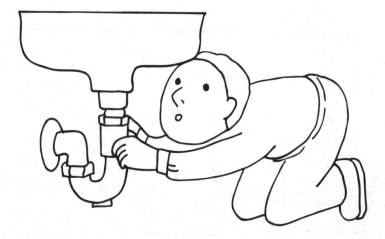

18

Wonderful Workers

Listen to the rhyme. Can you say the rhyme?

The  firefighter comes and puts out the fire.

The  mechanic's the one who fixes our tire.

The  mail carrier brings us a box or a letter

The  doctor's the one who helps us feel better.

The  baker wakes early and bakes us a bun.

Hooray for these workers who help everyone!

Draw lines to the matching workers.

FS132903 My Neighborhood

Name _____

Skill: Identifying
community helpers

Ready for Riddles

Listen to each riddle.
Cut and paste the matching worker in the correct place.

I bring letters to your family.
Who am I?

I have a big truck with a loud siren. Who am I?

I help cars go safely.
Who am I?

You might come to me when you are sick. Who am I?

© Frank Schaffer Publications, Inc.   20   FS132903 My Neighborhood

On the Road

Cut out the things that go on the road
and paste them on the picture.

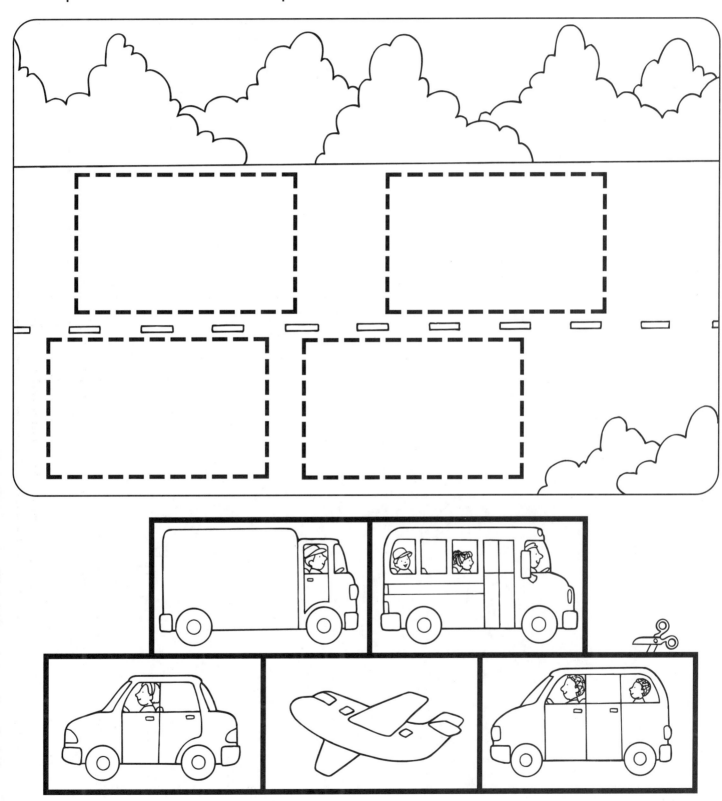

Name _____

Going Home

Help the family get home.

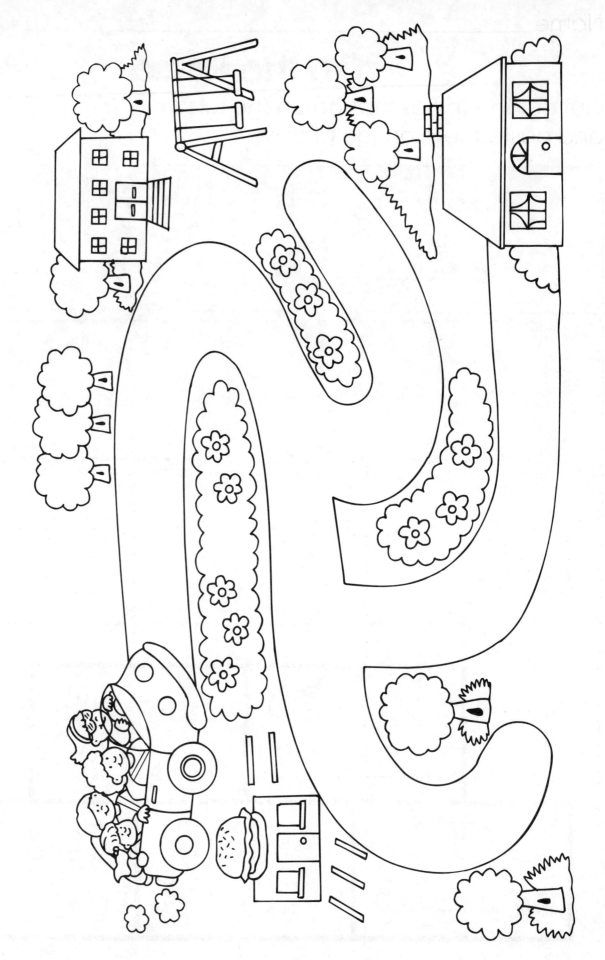

FS132903 My Neighborhood

Name _____

In the Water

Cut out the things that go on the water and paste them on the picture.

Get Ready to Land

Help the plane get to the airport.

AIRPORT

24

In the Air

Cut out the things that go in the air and
paste them on the picture.

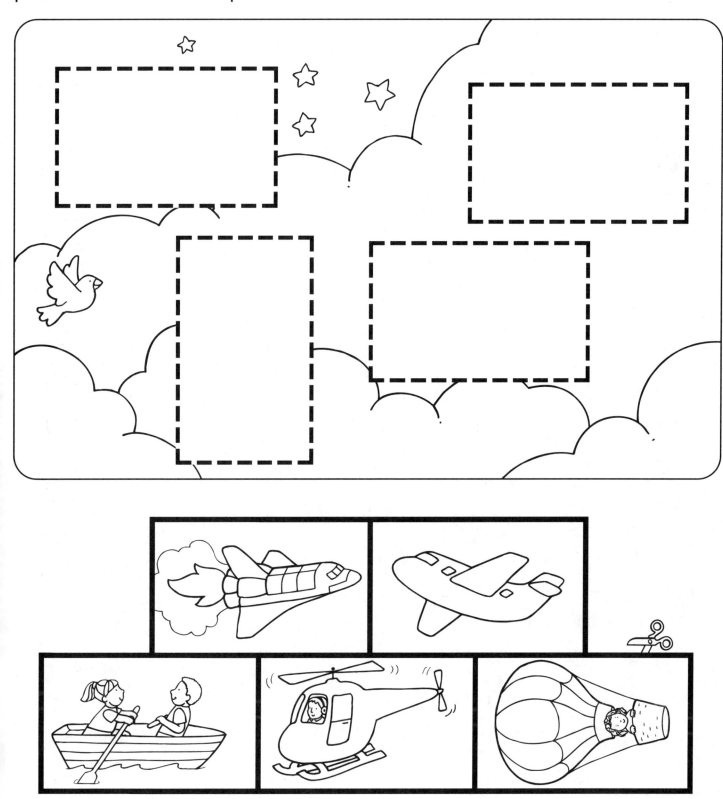

FS132903 My Neighborhood

Skill: Picture details

Clickety-clack!

Cut out the train and the tracks.
Fold the train to make it stand up.

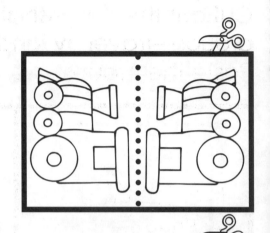

Make the train travel along the
tracks from Start to Finish.

Name the things you see along
the way.

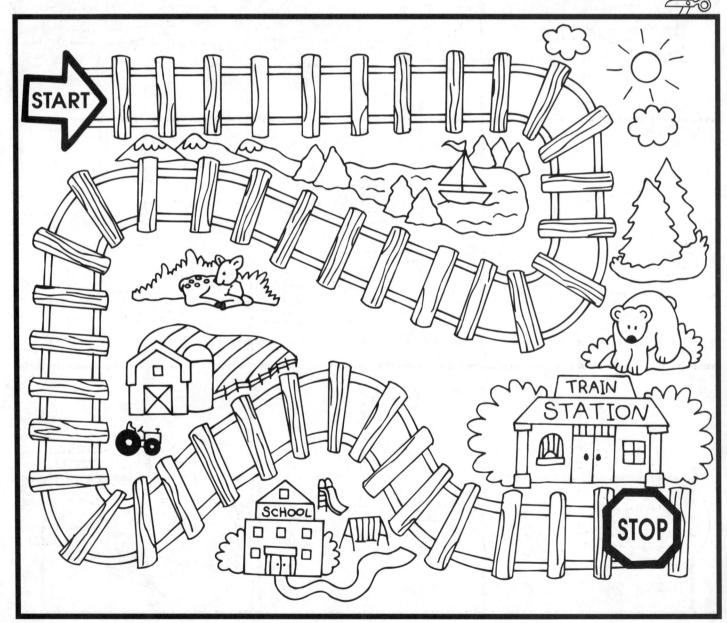

26 FS132903 My Neighborhood

Land, Water, or Air?

Cut out the pictures and put them into three groups—travel **by land**, **by water**, or **by air**. Paste the groups to another sheet of paper.

All Aboard!

Color and cut out the train cars. Listen to your teacher for directions.

Teacher: Have students place the cards faceup and find the card with the engine. Next, have the students place the cards in this order after the engine—girl, boy, lady, man, and caboose. Then ask the students questions such as *Who is behind the engineer? Who is in front of the little boy? Who is between the boy and the man?* To change the activity, simply have the students place the passenger cards in a different order.

FS132903 My Neighborhood

Name _____

The Wheels on the Bus

Color and cut out the cards. Tape them to craft sticks.
Use them as puppets to sing "The Wheels on the Bus."

Teacher: These cards illustrate the following verses: *The wheels on the bus go round and round; The horn on the bus goes
beep, beep, beep; The coins on the bus go clink, clink, clink; The people on the bus go up and down; The babies on the bus
go waa, waa, waa; The parents on the bus go shh, shh, shh; The wipers on the bus go swish, swish, swish.*

29

Ways to Go

Use this page with page 31.
Cut and staple the pages to make a book.

I Like to Ride

I like to ride in a car.
Honk! Honk!
Do you?

1

I like to ride in a bus.
Beep! Beep!
Do you?

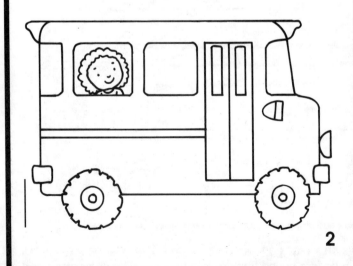

2

I like to ride in a truck.
Vroom! Vroom!
Do you?

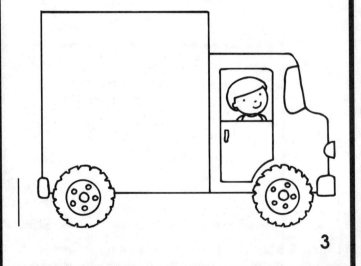

3

Ways to Go

Use this page with page 30.
Cut and staple the pages to make a book.

I like to ride on a boat.
Toot! Toot!
Do you?

4

I like to ride on a train.
Choo! Choo!
Do you?

5

I like to ride in a plane.
Zoom! Zoom!
Do you?

6

I like to ride
All kinds of things!
Do you?

7

31   FS132903 My Neighborhood

Can You Find These Things?

Find and color these things.